25 St. Margaret Patten's.
26 St. Mary at Hill.
27 St. Botolph's Aldgate.
28 St. Dunstan's in ye. East.

29 Billingsgate.
30 St. Olaves.
31 Bear Key.
32 Allhallow's Barkin.

33 Custom House.
34 Tower Hill.
35 The Armory.
36 Tower Stairs.

37 St. Georges in ye. East.
38 Tower.
39 St. Ann's Limehouse.
40 London Bridge.

Garden Court, Middle Temple, London.

9	St. Benedict's.	13 St. Michael's Crooked Lane.	17 St. Botolph's near Bishop's gate.	21 St. Magnus.
10	St. Clements Eastcheap.	14 Fishmongers Hall.	18 St. Bennet's.	22 St. Dionas back.
11	St. Edmond the King's.	15 Allhallow's.	19 Water Tower.	23 St. George's.
12	St. Michael's Cornhill.	16 St. Peter's Cornhill.	20 Monument.	24 Christ's Ch. Spitt.

Leads of St. Mary Overy's Church) & Engraved by S. & N. Buck, is Published according to Act of Parliament, Sept. 11th.

83 Old Street Church.
84 St Lawrence Jewry.
85 St Martin's.
86 Waterman's Hall.

87 Coleharbour Stairs.
88 Allhallow's.
89 St Stephen's Walbrook.
90 Mansion House.

1 St Swithin's.
2 St Margaret's Lothbury.
3 St Christopher's.
4 St Mary ab-Church.

5 St Mary Woolnoth.
6 St Bartholomew's.
7 Royal Exchange.
8 Old Swan Stairs.

This Drawing, taken from the West par

Dowgate Stairs.	75 St Mary le Bow.	78 Allhallows Stairs.	81 St Mary's Aldermanbury.
St Mary Alder Mary.	76 Steel Yard Stairs.	79 St Antholin's.	82 { St Michael's
St Michael Col Arts Hill.	77 St Alban's Woodstreet.	80 St Stephen's Coleman Str.	Bassingshaw.

1. Garden Court, Middle Temple, London.

61 St Nicholas Cole Abby.
62 St Pauls Cathedral.
63 St Michael's Queen-Hithe.

64 Three Crane Stairs.
65 St Austin's.
66 Christ Church.

67 St Mildred's.
68 St James's Garlick-Hill.
69 St Mathew's.

70 { St Vedest alias.
     St Foster's.
71 Allhallow's Breadstreet.

eads of St Mary Overy's Church) & Engraved by S. & N. Buck, is Published according to Act of Parliament, Sept. 11th 17

49 Fleet Ditch.	52 Puddle Dock.	55 Trig Stairs.	58 Queen-Hithe
50 St Sepulchres.	53 Pauls-Wharf.	56 St Bennets.	59 St Mary Son
51 Black Friers Stairs.	54 St Ann's Black Friers.	57 St Martin's Ludgate.	60 St Mary Ma

This Drawing, taken (from the West p

43 St Dunstan's.   45 Dorset-Stairs.   47 St Bride's.
44 White Friers-Stairs.   46 St Andrew's, Holborn.   48 Bridewel.

Garden Court, Middle Temple, London.

37 St. Clements.
38 Arundel-Stairs.
39 Efsex-Stairs.
40 Temple-Stairs.
41 Middle Temple
42 Temple-Church

...use, opposite to St. Bride's Church) & Engraved by S. & N. Buck, is Published according to Act of Parliament, Sept. 11th 1

31 *Somerset House.*   33 *S.t Mary le Strand.*   35 *Surrey-Stairs.*
32 *S.t George's, Bloomsbury.*   34 *Strand-Bridge.*   36 *Norfolk-Street.*

This Drawing, taken (from M.r Everard's Sum...

26 St Pauls, CoventGarden.
27 Savoy.
28 St Giles's.
29 Somerset Stairs.
30 {Part of Somerset
House.

C. 1. Garden Court, Middle Temple, London.

ford Stairs. 20 S.ᵗ Martin's.   22 Durham Yard.   24 Salisbury

Lyon Stairs. 21 York Stairs.   23 Ivy Bridge.   25 S.ᵗ Ann's,

House, opposite to Somerset House) & Engraved by S. & N. Buck, is Published according to Act of Parliament, Sept. 11ᵗʰ

12 *Part of the Treasury.*   14 *White Hall Stairs.*   16 *Admiralty.*
13 *White Hall.*   15 *Horse Guards.*   17 *S.ₜ James's.*

This Drawing, taken (from M.ᵣ Wats...

8 St. Margaret's.

9 Manchester Stairs.

10 Privy garden Stairs.

11 Part of ye Treasury.

...den Court, Middle Temple, London.

4 St John's.
5 Parliament House.
6 Westminster Hall.
7 Westminster Abby.

House, opposite to York House) & Engraved by S. & N. Buck, is Published according to Act of Parliament, Sept. 11th 1749.

The New Bridge at Westminster.

2 *Millbank.*
3 *Horse Ferry.*
This Drawing, taken (from Mr. Scheve's

PANORAMA OF
LONDON
1749

From an original engraving made by the Buck Brothers in 1749

Contemporary notes by John Wellsman in 1972

SIDGWICK & JACKSON
LONDON

ISBN 0 283 97912 7
Printed in Great Britain by
Wood Westworth & Co. Ltd.
for Sidgwick and Jackson Limited
1 Tavistock Chambers, Bloomsbury Way
London WC1A 2SG

PANORAMA OF LONDON
1749
Commentary by J. S. Wellsman

LONDON was at its most splendid when the Buck Brothers drew this panorama in the middle of the eighteenth century. Eighty years before, the Great Fire had swept away the medieval city, fascinating in its untidiness, though perhaps only in retrospect. Wren had built his Renaissance churches and great cathedral, and the aristocracy and gentry had deserted the narrow lanes of the City to build their classically-proportioned mansions in the hitherto undeveloped West End of the town. The Industrial Revolution with its menace of smoke and patina of grime was at least half a century away. The air was clean and fish still swam under Old London Bridge.

London is, in many ways, an ideal subject to be shown in panorama. With the single exception of Southwark Cathedral and a few minor though interesting sites, no important buildings have existed south of the river between the Tower and Westminster (this just excludes Lambeth Palace). So the whole town can be viewed from the South Bank. Also, London is, very conveniently, built round a curve of the Thames which helps the artist considerably in avoiding distortion of perspective.

The panorama was published in 1749, but it does not represent London as it was that year in the same way that a photograph of a scene reproduces its exact appearance at a precise moment in time. Such an extensive drawing must have taken many years to prepare; changes would occur after the plate for a particular section had been engraved and it was very difficult, if not impossible, to make later corrections on the plates. There are several buildings that had been demolished by the time the complete work was published. The opposite was also true as Westminster Bridge is shown almost complete, but was not, in fact, ready until well over a year later. But, in spite of the fact that the panorama does not represent London at any particular moment in time, I have assumed in a general way that it does in order to simplify comparison of dates.

Very little is known of the brothers Samuel and Nathaniel Buck, the authors of this work. They made a great number of engravings of castles, abbeys and miscellaneous ruins about the country as well as a number of London scenes during the 1730s. Their drawings show a firm grasp of architectural structure and line but display a lack of enthusiasm when introducing figures, animals and so on. Nathaniel died about 1760, but his brother Samuel who lived in the Strand opposite St Clement Danes, died in poverty in 1779 and was buried in that churchyard.

*　　*　　*

Starting at the Westminster end, the panorama begins in open country of fields and trees rising gently from the river to Camden and Notting Hill. The first buildings to be seen along the river bank are a tiny group of houses about two miles away amongst which can be seen a tower like a modern cooling tower. This is the Chelsea Water Works, situated where Chelsea Bridge now stands.

But London really begins with the fine row of houses on Millbank. The largest and most westerly was Grosvenor House, the home of the Grosvenor family, then Marquises and, later in Queen Victoria's reign, Dukes of Westminster.

At the east end of this row is the Middlesex landing stage of the Horse Ferry, the only one in London (the Surrey landing stage was just above Lambeth Palace). In the middle of the river is the Horse Ferry itself with a carriage and pair aboard, but the new Westminster Bridge, the major feature of this section of the panorama, made the Horse Ferry redundant. The Archbishop of Canterbury who was the proprietor of the Horse Ferry was paid £3,000 as compensation for loss of fees. It was while crossing at this ferry in his flight from William of Orange, that James II threw into the Thames the Great Seal of England; it was fished up by chance from the river-bed a few months later.

The bridge is referred to as 'the New Bridge at Westminster' and to Londoners it was new in more senses than one. Until it was built, London Bridge was the only one below Kingston, and although the need for more bridges in London had long been recognized, the watermen, the taxi-drivers of the time, had successfully opposed the building of new bridges. The depiction of the bridge in an almost complete state is one of the anachronistic features of the panorama as it was not opened to the public until 18 November 1750, fourteen months after the publication date of the panorama which must have been drawn a considerable time before this date (11 September 1749). The only easily detectable sign of its incompleteness is that only a few of the hoods are in position over the semi-circular seats placed over the piers. Each hood bore a lamp but none of these are shown. In the bottom left-hand corner some masons can be seen at work on stones for the bridge.

St John's (Smith Square) (No. 4) Archer's Baroque church is prominently shown. This church, nicknamed 'Queen Anne's Footstool', and described at the time by Lord Chesterfield as being like an elephant lying on its back, had been seriously damaged by fire in 1742. Almost exactly 200 years later it was gutted by the Luftwaffe.

Westminster Abbey shows the two towers at long last completed in 1740 by Wren and his successors. The re-facing of the whole exterior, with the exception of the Henry VII chapel had also just been finished.

The Privy Garden Stairs (No. 10), lead to a terrace garden built by Wren for Queen Mary, wife and co-sovereign of William III. It was built in 1692 and a far more imposing flight of stairs is shown at the right-hand end of the terrace; the remains of these can still be seen on the river side of the new Ministry of Defence building by Horse Guards Avenue. It is a striking indication of how far the river was pushed back by the Victoria Embankment in 1870.

The clock tower of the Horseguards (No. 15) is that of the old building built in 1641 and now, a century later, in a grievous condition. Its archway entrance to St. James's Park was considered unsafe for carriages and the guards on duty were constantly in danger from falling masonry. It was pulled down in 1750 and the present building erected.

Scotland Yard was a rather shapeless mass of buildings which can be seen beneath the weather-vane of the Admiralty (No. 16). It was named after the London residence of the Kings of Scotland, and lay between the present Northumberland Avenue and Horse Guards Avenue. Inigo Jones, Milton, and Christopher Wren all lived here at some time but its most famous association is, of course, with the Metropolitan Police who had their first headquarters here.

Just below and to the right of the steeple of St James's (No. 17) can be seen three turrets, each with a weather-vane. A fourth can be seen to the left of the steeple. These turrets mark the four corners of Northumberland House built in 1605, which stood at the north end of Northumberland Avenue. It had been known as Northampton House and Suffolk House before being named Northumberland House in the first half of the eighteenth century. Its ownership had passed by marriage through various families before becoming the town house of the Dukes of Northumberland. It was compulsorily purchased in 1873 to make way for the building of Northumberland Avenue. The famous lead lion, badge of the Dukes of Northumberland, placed over the Strand entrance was then removed to Syon House, Isleworth.

The York Watergate (No. 21) can be seen today in the Embankment Gardens to the east of Charing Cross railway station. It was built in 1626 – some say by Inigo Jones, though this is far from certain – as a river entrance to York House which had just been acquired by George Villiers, Duke of Buckingham. It is another landmark showing how far the river has been pushed back. The tall conical tower a little to the west of the watergate is the tower of the York Buildings waterworks for the supply of water to the West End. The handsome house between the waterworks and the watergate is the Salt Office from which the Salt Tax of the time was administered.

On the skyline above Durham Yard (No. 22) can be seen a long building considerably larger than any of its neighbours. The most noticeable feature is the row of eleven chimneys on its roof. This is the New Exchange and is another anachronism as it was pulled down in 1737, twelve years before the published date of the Panorama. It stood at the south side of the Strand opposite Bedford Street. It opened in 1608 as a second Royal Exchange but failed to gain any popularity until the time of James II when the West End was becoming fashionable, especially Covent Garden. It contained the shops of modish drapers and milliners as well as many other commercial establishments, and was quite a resort of Society. After Queen Anne's death it declined in popularity.

Notice the frequency of river stairs all along the river bank round which cluster numbers of small boats waiting for passengers. In the sixteenth century the stairs were called bridges and two, Ivy Bridge (No. 23) and Strand Bridge (No. 34), still retain that name in the Panorama. Sixty years later a bridge in the modern sense was built near the Strand Bridge Stairs and was itself called Strand Bridge at first, but, after a famous victory of the time, was renamed Waterloo Bridge. A hundred years after the Panorama was published, virtually all these river stairs had vanished as can be seen in the Vizetelly Panorama*; the building of the bridges and the invention of the steam engine had destroyed the river trade.

The Savoy (No. 27), a palace built by the Earl of Savoy and Richmond in 1245, was in a ruinous state at this time. It was being used as an army recruiting centre, barracks and military prison; the King's Printing House was also here for a time. Sixty years later the rambling building was pulled down for the constructon of Waterloo Bridge, and all that remains today is the Chapel of the Savoy built in 1505.

Somerset House (No. 31) was built by the Protector Duke of Somerset in the middle of the sixteenth century, and had become the traditional home of the Queens of England during Stuart times. The old building was pulled down in 1776 and replaced by the present Somerset House to provide accommodation for government offices and learned societies. As compensation, Queen Charlotte, wife of George III, was given Buckingham House in St James's Park which, as a palace, has since become the London home for the Royal Family.

The building immediately to the west of the Surrey Stairs (No. 35) is the Hackney Coach Office, from which were licensed all the coaches in England. The number of coaches in London was limited to seven hundred and a licence cost £50 for twenty-one years as well as a yearly fee of £4. To hire a coach cost 1s. 6d. (7½p) for the first hour, and 1s. (5p) an hour after that.

Essex Stairs (No. 39) marks the boundary between Westminster and the City.

The church of St Dunstan's in the West (No. 43) shown here, was pulled down in 1829 and replaced by the present church. But the two giants in their little Greek temple which today strike the hours from this church came from the old church on which they were placed in 1671.

With the exception of St Paul's Cathedral, St Andrew's, Holborn, (No. 46) is the largest of Wren's churches, rebuilt, not as a result of the Fire of London but because

*Published by Sidgwick & Jackson in 1972 as *The Grand Panorama of London*

it was in a bad state of repair at the time. Benjamin Disraeli was baptized a Christian in this church in 1817 at the age of twelve.

St Bride's spire (No. 47) is considered one of Wren's greatest works and is also his tallest steeple. Probably due to its great height it was to be struck by lightning in 1764 and considerably damaged. When it was rebuilt the spire was shortened by eight feet to 226 feet. It was this accident that drew considerable attention to the necessity for lightning conductors; Benjamin Franklin had recently been investigating this very problem.

Bridewell (No. 48) which stood on the west side of what is now New Bridge Street was a prison for petty criminals, vagabonds, prostitutes, and the like. The flogging of these was something of a public spectacle during the eighteenth century.

The Fleet Ditch (No. 49), as its name here implies, was not regarded as being either useful (except as a sewer) or ornamental. It had already been covered over down to where Ludgate Circus is now, and in 1766 the remainder down to the river was to be covered. Until the seventeenth century, the Fleet had been an important river of commerce but, due to silting and neglect, it had deteriorated into little more than a ditch. The attractive little bridge, modelled on the Rialto in Venice, can be seen crossing the Fleet from Bridewell to Blackfriars.

St Sepulchre's (No. 50) was the only City church damaged in the Fire of London and not rebuilt by Wren, who was rather annoyed about it. During the eighteenth century, the Bellman of the Church would cross to Newgate Prison (where the Old Bailey stands now), ring his bell outside the condemned cell, and recite a verse reminding the inmates, somewhat unnecessarily one would have thought, of their fate next morning. And this took place at midnight and in the name of Charity! The rather imposing house appearing immediately below St Sepulchre's tower was a private house but of no particular interest.

The tower numbered 54 is named as 'St Ann's Blackfriars' but I believe that this is incorrect. This church was destroyed in the Great Fire and was not rebuilt; towers of burnt churches often survived but I cannot trace any record of this tower having survived eighty years nor does it appear on contemporary maps. Secondly, the church stood within 150 yards of the Fleet river and the position on the Panorama does not seem to fit this. Thirdly, the tower resembles that of St Andrew in the Wardrobe which was rebuilt but is not named by the Buck Brothers. Curiously, Vizetelly's panorama seems to make the same mistake; this may have occurred because the two parishes united after the Fire and perhaps also because of the slight similarity of the names.

The remaining stretch of the Panorama must be regarded as the most impressive of its entire length. To appreciate it fully it must be viewed as a whole, for the skyline of the City from the Cathedral to the Tower appears as a splendid procession of towers and spires marching westward, led by the great church of St Paul's with no ugly interruptions except, perhaps, for the attic storeys of the Mansion House and they, surrounded closely by spires, appear as if to add to the simile, like prisoners under guard.

Queenhithe (No. 58) is probably the oldest feature of the river-side in London. Although not depicted very clearly here, this small rectangular harbour which still exists today may have been constructed originally by the Romans. In the Middle Ages it belonged to various queens and its name arises from this. In early times, Queenshithe and Billingsgate were the two principal ports of London but, as sea-going ships became larger and the difficulties of passing London Bridge consequently became greater, the traffic at Queenshithe dwindled to little more than local river trade.

From Three Crane Stairs (No. 64) the Lord Mayor of London embarked on his barge to be rowed in state up to Westminster Hall, there to take his oath of office before the Barons of the Exchequer. Much further west, between the mouth of the Fleet and the Temple two state barges can be seen. The leading one flies the City flag and may be intended to depict the Lord Mayor's State Barge, though it bears little resemblance to the actual barge. Water processions ended in 1857. It was customary to return from Westminster on land; in 1711 the last Lord Mayor returned on horse-back and thereafter the famous State Coach was used. Southwark Bridge was built at Three Crane Stairs.

Immediately to the west of Dowgate Stairs (No. 72) lies Dowgate Wharf, the last remaining visible sign of the Wallbrook stream which flowed southwards from Moorfields, under the City wall and down to this point. It was on the east bank of the Wallbrook that the Temple of Mithras was discovered in 1954.

St Mary Aldermary (No. 73) is perhaps the most unusual of Wren's churches. A Mrs Rogers left £5,000 for its restoration after the Great Fire on condition that it was rebuilt exactly as it had been before the Fire. Whether Wren was able to comply completely is not certain but the result is well worth seeing.

St Michael Colarts Hill (No. 74) is misnamed and this should read 'College Hill', though the title of this church is usually given as 'St Michael Paternoster Royal'. This was Richard Whittington's church and in his will, he left money for its support and for an almshouse for the poor of the parish. He was buried three times in this church; first on his death in 1423, secondly, during the reign of Edward VI after his grave had been disturbed because it was thought that treasure had been buried with him, and thirdly in the reign of Queen Mary to inter him more decently.

St Mary le Bow (No. 75) with its fine tower has been famous for its bells for centuries, for it was in the middle of the fifteenth century that the City Council ordered that the curfew should be rung from this church each evening at nine o'clock after which the taverns were to close. It was, of course, because the City curfew was rung from here, that the true Cockney or Londoner must be born within sound of these bells. The bells were destroyed with the church in the Great Fire, and the full peal of ten bells was not completely replaced until 1762. The church derives its name from the fact that the old Norman church was built on a foundation of stone arches or bows and these still exist and can be seen. Wren used these arches to support his church but he had to find a new foundation for the tower. To do this, he dug eighteen feet down when he came to a Roman roadway, one of the very few to be known with certainty within the City. He found it to be four feet thick, of brick and rubble, and strong enough to bear the weight of his tower.

St Stephen Walbrook (No. 89) is one of the finest Wren church interiors – the exterior is not remarkable – and his only domed church apart from St Paul's. In the Panorama this dome seems to have been detached and removed some distance from the tower which appears in its correct position just south of the Mansion House.

Building the Mansion House (No. 90), official residence of the Lord Mayor, was begun in 1739 but, because the ground was found to be so waterlogged, it was not completed until 1753. All that can be seen here are the two attic storeys, known at the time as the Mare's Nest and Noah's Ark. The latter was taken down in 1795 but the Mare's Nest remained until 1842.

The Royal Exchange (No. 7) was the second Exchange to be built here. The original building, founded by Sir Thomas Gresham, dated from 1566 but this was burnt in the Great Fire, and rebuilt, not by Wren, but by Mr Edward Jerman, Surveyor of the City of London. This building was destroyed by fire in 1838 and the present building was opened in 1844 by Queen Victoria. The grasshopper weather-vane is said to be the original which stood over the first Royal Exchange.

Fishmongers' Hall (No. 14), rebuilt after the Fire, was to be pulled down in 1825 to make way for the New London Bridge. The present Hall was completed in 1834. The actor, Doggett, a member of the Fishmongers' Company, instituted in 1721 the annual race for a Coat and Badge. The race, still competed for today, starts from Old Swan Stairs (No. 8) just to the west of Fishmongers' Hall, and ends at the Swan, Chelsea.

Of all London's historic features, London Bridge has always been the most famous, excelling even the Tower of London, and the lineage of its predecessors is as old as the City itself. But it is the London Bridge seen here that is the London Bridge of fame and legend. It was the largest of all bridges bearing houses, and neither the Ponte Vecchio of Florence or the Port-au-Change of Paris could compare with it. Its construction began in 1176 and was completed in 1209 together with its original houses and a beautiful little Gothic chapel in which the builder, Peter of Colechurch, was buried. He did not survive to see his work completed. The bridge was built on nineteen piers supporting twenty arches, including a drawbridge though this had ceased to be used as such by the end of the sixteenth century. The bows of a small boat with one oarsman visible can be seen under the disused drawbridge span. The enormous bulk of the nineteen piers so restricted the tidal flow of the river that when the tide was running, the difference in the height of water on either side of the bridge could be as much as five feet. This restriction was also the cause of the river freezing over in very cold weather. To the west of the northern end, is the Water Tower of the Bridge Waterworks (No. 19). This successful project was begun in 1580 using a waterwheel under the first arch to drive the pump. A second wheel in the next arch was added shortly afterwards, and by the end of the seventeenth century, four waterwheels were in use, the last of which can be seen. The buildings on the bridge were in their final state of delapidation. The houses which are shown here above the waterwheel as far as the first break in the buildings (which was known as 'The Square') had actually been demolished in 1745 and a very plain range of buildings designed by George Dance had replaced them. But by 1762 all the houses on the bridge had been taken down together with the waterworks and several of the piers removed to improve the flow of the river. Seventy years later, the bridge was completely pulled down and replaced by the bridge recently sold to the U.S.A.

St Peter Cornhill (No. 16) claims to be the oldest foundation in the City and declares that it was founded by St Helen, mother of the Emperor Constantine. There was also a claim in the sixteenth century that, before the arrival of St Augustine, St Peter's had been the cathedral church of the Archbishop of all England. The organ dates from 1681 and Mendelssohn played on it in 1840 and 1841.

The Monument (No. 20) to commemorate the Fire of London was put up where the Fire started. It was designed and built by Wren, though not exactly as he had wanted it to be. It took six years to erect and was completed in 1677. The inscription on the base originally contained words blaming the 'Papists' for starting the Fire but these were erased by the Catholic James II. When the Protestant William of Orange succeeded him, the words were re-cut but were finally erased in 1831.

St Magnus the Martyr (No. 21) was destroyed by the Great Fire and rebuilt by Wren. Soon after 1760, when the bridge was stripped of its houses, a pathway was made under the tower and on to the bridge, which enabled the roadway to be widened considerably. The original paving stones are still there. Until recently, St Magnus and its churchyard bordered the river, and in the fifteenth century the priests of this church were reprimanded for neglecting their services by fishing in the river. The organ dates from 1712 and is, I am told, the first swell organ to be made. The woodwork in this church is very fine and Pevsner, in his *Buildings of England*, describes it as 'one of the richest ensembles in the City'.

St Dunstan's in the East (No. 28), was partly destroyed in the Great Fire and restored by Wren who kept the body of the church much as it had been but completely rebuilt the tower with his striking design of four flying buttresses supporting a spire. Wren's daughter is traditionally associated with this church. One story says that she designed the tower. Another, more dramatic, claims that after sceptics had maintained that the buttresses would collapse when the scaffolding was removed, she stood beneath the tower when the supports were taken down, to show her faith in her father's skill. The body of the church was completely rebuilt in 1817 by Laing who had built the nearby Custom House, but this was destroyed in the Second World War though, fortunately, Wren's tower still stands.

Billingsgate (No. 29) had been the principal fish wharf of London from time immemorial, though in earlier days it had shared the trade with Queenhithe. But Billingsgate at this time was not only a fish wharf; Strype, in his Survey of London and Westminster of 1720, described it as '. . . a harbour for small vessels which here arrive with fish, salt, oranges, lemons, onions and several other commodities and in the summer season with abundance of cherries from Kent. Likewise wheat at Smarts Key. And these stairs at Billingsgate are very much resorted unto by the Gravesend watermen, this being the noted place to land and take water for that and other eastern towns down the river. And here coalmen and woodmongers meet every morning about 8 or 9 o'clock, this place being their Exchange for the coal trade'.

St Olave, Hart Street (No. 30) was regarded by Pepys as his own parish church and he was buried here in the vaults with his wife who had died thirty-four years before him. The skulls, which still adorn the gateway to the churchyard in Seething Lane, caused Dickens to refer to this church as 'St Ghastly Grim'.

All Hallows, Barking (No. 32), escaped the fire and the tower provided Pepys with an excellent view of its progress. This tower has the distinction of being the only surviving building in London to be erected during the Commonwealth period. The church, one of the oldest in the City, was gravely damaged in the Second World War but has been restored as closely as possible to the original.

The Custom House (No. 33) shown here had been built by Ripley about thirty years before. There has been, to our knowledge, a Custom House at Billingsgate since 1382 and as customs had been collected here long before that date, there may have been even earlier ones. It has always been a most important collection point as only the smallest seagoing vessels could pass the drawbridge of London Bridge. Ripley's Custom House was the fourth to be built, the third having been built by Wren and burnt down in 1718. Ripley's building was itself burnt down in 1814 and was rebuilt by Laing, and this Custom House has survived with some modification to the present day.

Tower Hill (No. 34) is most famous as being the site of the scaffold and block at which offenders were beheaded for what we would now call political crimes. Sir Thomas More, Chancellor of Henry VIII, and the rebellious Duke of Monmouth, illegitimate son of Charles II, are two of the most well known to be executed here. Two years before the date of the Panorama, the last public beheading at Tower Hill took place, that of Lord Lovat for his association with the Scottish rebellion. This was also the last beheading to take place anywhere in England. Lord Lovat, together with two other Scottish peers who were beheaded two years before him are remembered today in the name of a public house, 'The Three Lords', in the Minories near by.

St George in the East (No. 37) was built by Hawkesmoor in 1723 and was gutted in the Second World War. It is situated off the Ratcliffe Highway in Stepney. It is doubtful whether it really was visible from the viewpoint of this section and one wonders why the Buck Brothers took the trouble to draw it in and identify it. Since it is here it may be of interest to note that about a hundred years later it was the scene of a bitter dispute between two ministers, one High Church, the other Low Church. The Low Church party used every device of rowdyism, including musical instruments, rotten vegetables and savage dogs to desecrate the services held by the High Church Rector. In the end, nobody won.